Published by
Tutor Master Services

David Malindine

B.A.(Hons), M.A.(London), P.G.C.E.,
Adv.Dip.Ed.(Open), R.S.A. Cert.

Tutor Master Services
61 Ashness Gardens
Greenford
Middlesex
UB6 0RW

david@tutormaster-services.co.uk
www.tutormaster-services.co.uk

Acknowledgements

Thanks to Christine Malindine for preparing this book
and to Martyn Clarke for proofreading the scripts

For

Zhee Laine, Zhee Nedd and Zhee Gienne

First Published 2015

© David Malindine 2015

ISBN: 978-0-9555909-8-6

Printed by G.H.Smith & Son, Design Printing Publishing, Easingwold, York

Tel: 01347 821329 Fax: 01347 822576

Web: www.ghsmith.com

Contents

Who this book is for

The ability to read and make meaning from written information are crucial skills for students of all ages. These skills are tested regularly in state, grammar and independent/private schools.

When children move from primary school to secondary school at the end of Year 6 aged 11 years, some parents may wish their child to take examinations in order to achieve a place at a grammar or independent/private school. Because the entry requirements to such schools vary from place to place around the country, it is important for parents to prepare themselves by doing some research about the schools that they may wish their child to attend.

Schools publish their entry requirements for students moving schools at age 11+ and it is important that parents find out about the admissions policies of the school and any examinations that the school may set, in order that they can prepare their children properly.

Examinations in English tend to be a reading passage accompanied by either a multiple choice or standard answer comprehension test, plus a piece of written creative writing, composition or essay.

For multiple choice answer tests, answers are recorded by ticking or marking a box on an answer sheet. For standard comprehension tests answers are written in an answer book.

It is my experience as a tutor that many parents enter children for more than one type of school. The Tutor Master papers take this into account by providing separate books with practice tests for both Multiple Choice English Comprehension and Standard English Comprehension papers.

This book has been written with the aim of helping students practise their comprehension skills as a way of improving their abilities to understand written information.

The tests contained in this book have been prepared for children in school years 4, 5 and 6, ages 8 – 11 years old. As well as being helpful for general revision and practice, these comprehension tests are written to particularly assist students who are preparing for entrance examinations at 11+ for grammar schools and independent schools.

How to use this book

This book contains important, practical advice on the best ways to approach standard comprehension tests and how to write effective and purposeful answers. The book also provides tips and advice for writing compositions/essays. These are writing tests that cover aspects of creative writing such as stories, reports and letters.

Five standard comprehension tests are provided, each with a reading passage followed by questions that are answered by the students on the papers provided.

Each of the five comprehension tests is accompanied by a composition/essay test that provides a choice of two tasks for the student to attempt.

A clear, helpful and detailed marking scheme is provided for both the comprehension test and compositions to enable an accurate assessment to be made of each student's performance.

Tutor M aster Services

ENGLISH
Comprehension

Standard

Tips and Advice
for completing
Comprehensions and Compositions

Comprehension Tips

It is a good idea for the student to read through this advice with an adult before they begin the comprehension papers.

- Read the story passage carefully as it is important you understand it. Remember as much as you can. (It may help if you think of your brain as a sponge, soaking up as many details as you can!)

- Read the question carefully then do **exactly** as it says, e.g., if the question asks you to answer in your **own words**, make sure you do.

- Always answer in **full sentences** unless you are told not to.

- It is important that you understand that you are allowed to go back and check the reading passage to help you answer the questions. In fact it is **essential** to use the reading passage to help. This exam is not a memory test.

- When you answer, use words and phrases from the passage as **evidence** to back up your ideas.

- If you use words from the passage as evidence to help explain your answer, make sure you put the words you use in quotation marks (" ").

- If a question asks you to explain a word and you are not sure what it means, go back to the passage and read the sentences that come before and after the word you need to explain. Use the **context** in which the word is used to have your best guess.

- Look at the marks being given for each question. Make sure you give enough **evidence** and **details** to get the number of marks being given.

- If the question has two parts make sure you give a two part answer to cover each part of the question.

- Present your work as neatly as you can and make sure you spell correctly, especially when words you are using are copied from the passage or question.

- Always try to write an answer for every question. If you do not answer you will lose marks. Always have a guess if you are unsure as you never know, you may be correct!

- Some questions are about grammar, spellings and parts of speech. To find out more about words and their meanings my book, *Tutor Master helps you Learn English - A Literacy Dictionary*, contains lots of helpful definitions and examples.

Practical Advice

- Agree a suitable time and place where the practice test will be carried out. It is advisable for the student to conduct the test in a place where they can be supervised and timed by an adult and which will also be free from noise or distractions.

- Provide a clock that the student can see, several pencils, a ruler and an eraser. It is probably better to write answers in pencil so that any mistakes can be more easily corrected.

- As this is a practice situation it is probably helpful to read through the instructions on the front page with the student before they begin.

- Make sure the student understands what they have to do before they begin and give them the chance to ask any questions.

Tips for Writing Compositions

These are general guidelines only. For more detailed advice and practical help with story writing, see *Tutor Master helps you Write Stories Book 1* and *Tutor Master helps you Write Stories Book 2*.

- When choosing a story to write in an exam it is a good idea to choose the title that you may be able to write from your own experience. This makes it easier as you know how the story begins, what happens and how it ends.

- It is **very important** to make sure that the story you write is about the title you have chosen or been given.

- Examiners often prefer you to show your writing skills by making your story sound true, even if it is made up. Amazing, improbable adventure stories are often difficult to complete in the half hour of writing time available.

- Try to think how your story will end **before** you start to write. It is very important that you finish the story. If you already know how it will end you can quickly bring it to a conclusion if you find you are running out of time.

- It is a good idea to write your stories in the **past tense** as you will find it easier to maintain this throughout the story.

- Make sure your story has a clear **beginning** where you set the scene and introduce the main ideas – this should be fairly short, maybe just one paragraph. Make sure the **middle** part of your story is the longest part containing two, three or more paragraphs. **End** your story with a fairly short concluding paragraph.

- Begin a new paragraph each time you change the topic you are writing about.

- Be careful to punctuate your work using the rules for punctuating written work.

- Be careful to spell correctly, especially those words you know you find difficult.

- Try to include some **direct speech** correctly punctuated using the rules for punctuating direct speech.

- Write good descriptions using adjectives, adverbs and similes.

- Try to describe your **feelings** or the **feelings** of the characters you are writing about.

TutorMasterServices

ENGLISH
Comprehension
Standard Introductory
Paper 2A
40 minutes

Read the following carefully:

1. This paper is in two parts – a comprehension and a composition (story). You should spend about half an hour on each part.

2. Start this test when you are told to do so.

3. You should read the passage and then answer the questions about it. It is a good idea to look back at the passage to check your answers as many times as you want.

4. You should aim to finish all the questions.

5. Work as quickly and as carefully as you can.

6. You will have an extra 10 minutes reading time, 30 minutes to do the comprehension and 30 minutes for the composition.

Text © David Malindine

The right of David Malindine to be identified as author of this work has been asserted by him in accordance with the Copyright, Designs and Patents Act 1988.

Copyright © Tutor Master Services, 2015

Published by:

Tutor Master Services, 61 Ashness Gardens, Greenford, Middlesex UB6 0RW.

ISBN: 978-0-9555909-8-6

Read the passage below and answer the following questions carefully. It is a good idea to go back and check the passage to find your answers. Write your answers neatly on the answer sheet.

Aladdin

In a land far away to the East, there once lived a lazy lad named Aladdin. His father Qaseem had died of grief as his idle son made no attempt to mend his ways and lived as an impoverished ne'er-do-well.

One day a stranger visited the town where Aladdin lived and on meeting
5 Aladdin announced that he was Aladdin's long lost Uncle Mustafa. Aladdin and his mother were taken aback at this news as it had long been thought that Uncle Mustafa had died, but their misgivings were put aside when the stranger convinced them of his goodwill by making arrangements to set up young Aladdin as a merchant.

10 The very next day Aladdin and Mustafa set off to buy stock to begin their trading venture. They journeyed for a long while through the mountains until they halted in a narrow valley. After lighting a fire Mustafa produced some magic powder which he threw into the flames and in a flash of sparks and smoke a stone slab was revealed, and set in it was a large brass ring.
15 Mustafa pulled on the ring and the slab opened to reveal steps leading down to an underground cave filled with treasure. Mustafa promised Aladdin great wealth if he were to go down into the cave to retrieve an old oil lamp that would be found on an ancient stone table.

Aladdin was apprehensive at the thought of stepping down into the chamber
20 but was eventually won over by his uncle who offered him a special ring for protection in case of trouble.

Once inside the cave Aladdin picked his way carefully through the piles of treasures until he found the lamp. Picking it up, he carefully retraced his way and climbed the steps. As he was nearing the top his uncle demanded
25 the lamp, but as Aladdin was not yet safely out of the cave he refused. In a fit of anger Mustafa uttered some magic words, and the stone slab slammed shut. Aladdin was trapped.

Immediately Aladdin realised that Mustafa had tried to trick him and he was not his real uncle, but a wicked magician who had wanted to use Aladdin
30 for his own ends. Alone in the cave, Aladdin clasped his hands together in prayer and as he did so inadvertently rubbed the ring given to him by the evil Mustafa. At once, a genie appeared who was able to grant Aladdin his wish to be saved, and took him home to his mother.

Once at home Aladdin's mother was desperate for food and money as they
35 were very poor. Aladdin suggested that they sell the old lamp, but before he did so, decided to give it a quick polish. Instantly, a huge genie, more powerful than the first, appeared and informed them he was bound to do the bidding of the person in possession of the lamp.

With the aid of the genie of the lamp, Aladdin and his mother were able to

40 become rich and powerful by selling silverware conjured up by the genie of the lamp. Eventually, wealthy and prosperous, Aladdin married Princess Badroulbadour, the Sultan's daughter, and with the help of the genie moved into a palace far more magnificent than that of the Sultan himself.

One day however, the sinister magician returned to the town and tricked Aladdin's wife, who was unaware of the lamp's importance, by offering to

45 exchange "new lamps for old". Once in possession of the lamp he ordered the genie of the lamp to take the palace and the princess and magically transport them to his own city in a country far away.

Desperately sad, anxious and alone, Aladdin summoned the assistance of the genie of the ring. Although the genie of the ring had lesser power

50 and was unable to undo the magic of the genie of the lamp, he was able to magically transport Aladdin to the site of his palace and to his wife the Princess Badroulbadour.

When she laid eyes on Aladdin again the princess was delighted to see him and reassured him of her love for him. She told him that the dishonourable

55 magician had told her that Aladdin was long since dead and she should marry him now. Princess Badroulbadour had constantly refused him his wish and remained loyal to Aladdin.

To trick the evil magician, Aladdin and his princess hatched a cunning plan. They agreed that the princess would pretend to accept his marriage

60 requests. One night as they prepared to celebrate the forthcoming wedding Princess Badroulbadour persuaded the magician to go down to the wine cellar to bring back some fine wines to drink.

Bedazzled by her beauty and charms, the magician hurried off. Meanwhile the princess sprinkled some special powder that Aladdin had provided,

65 into a cup. On his return the magician poured out the wine and drank from the cup. Immediately, he fell down, quite dead!

Aladdin retrieved his magic lamp and asked the genie to restore things to the way they were. Soon the palace, with Aladdin and Princess Badroulbadour inside, was returned safely to the kingdom. The Sultan was overjoyed to

70 see his daughter safely returned. Aladdin was reunited with his mother, and they all lived happily ever after.

ANSWER SECTION

PLEASE WRITE YOUR FULL NAME HERE:

_____

MARKS

1. Paragraph 1 (lines 1 - 3), tells us that Aladdin did not like to work hard. Copy down the three phrases which tell us this.

3

   Phrase one …………………………………………………………………

   …………………………………………………………………………………

   Phrase two …………………………………………………………………

   …………………………………………………………………………………

   Phrase three …………………………………………………………………

   …………………………………………………………………………………

2. Complete the table below to show the relationships between the characters mentioned in this story. Choose names from the box below.

6

Magician; Sultan; Mustafa's nephew; Aladdin's wife; Uncle Mustafa; Qaseem

Name	Relationship
	Aladdin's father
Aladdin	
Uncle Mustafa	
	Aladdin's father-in-law
Princess Badroulbadour	
	Wicked Uncle

3. From paragraph 2 (lines 4 - 9), explain why Aladdin and his mother were surprised when the stranger announced that he was Aladdin's Uncle Mustafa.

2

…………………………………………………………………………………………

…………………………………………………………………………………………

…………………………………………………………………………………………

…………………………………………………………………………………………

4. Use information in paragraphs 2 and 3 to explain why Aladdin and his uncle set off on a long journey.

3

…………………………………………………………………………………………

…………………………………………………………………………………………

…………………………………………………………………………………………

…………………………………………………………………………………………

…………………………………………………………………………………………

5. The following is a list of events which happen in the paragraph 3 (lines 10 - 18). They have been mixed up. You must try to put them back in order by writing numbers 2 - 6 against each one. The first has been done for you.

5

Uncle Mustafa pulls on the ring. ………

Uncle Mustafa promised Aladdin great wealth. ………

Uncle Mustafa lit a fire. **1** ………

Steps were revealed. ………

Uncle Mustafa produced some magic powder. ………

A stone slab was revealed. ………

6. In paragraph 4 (lines 19 - 21), Aladdin was nervous about stepping into the chamber. Copy down the phrase that meant he was finally persuaded to do so.

2

....

....

....

....

7. Why does Aladdin not hand over the lamp he has found in the cave to his Uncle?

3

....

....

....

....

8. What is the outcome for Aladdin of not handing over the lamp to his Uncle?

3

....

....

....

....

9. In paragraphs 6, 7 and 8 (lines 28 - 43) Aladdin and his mother are helped by the Genie of the Ring and the Genie of the Lamp. In your own words explain how these two magical people assist them.

3

....

....

....

....

....

10. Copy out the phrase from the passage that means the same as, "your original lamp traded for a more modern one".

3

....

....

11. Pick out and write down the three feelings experienced by Aladdin after his wife and palace are taken away.

3

1)...

2)...

3)...

12. Put a ring around the word which is closest in meaning to the word "dishonourable" (line 54) as it is used in the passage.

2

    distinguished   decent   shameful   reputable

13. Put a ring around the word which is closest in meaning to the word "loyal" (line 57) as it is used in the passage.

2

    treacherous   false   traitorous   faithful

14. Put a ring around the word which is closest in meaning to the word "forthcoming" (line 60) as it is used in the passage.

2

    distant   far-off   impending   remote

15. Find and copy down from the passage words or phrases that mean the same as;

a) Princess Badroubadour always said no to the magician's marriage requests

2

Words or phrase ....

....

....

b) Aladdin and Princess Badroubadour devised a clever plot

2

Words or phrase ....

....

....

2

c) Bewitched by her attractiveness

Words or phrase ....

....

....

16. In the first and last paragraphs two phrases are used which suggest this story may
not be true. Copy them down.

a) ....

1

....

b) ....

1

....

TOTAL MARKS =   **50**

END OF QUESTIONS ON PART ONE

Tutor Master Services

ENGLISH
Composition/Essay

30 minutes
Total Marks: 50

Choose one of these to write

1. In the story we are told that the genie of the ring was able to magically transport Aladdin to the palace where Princess Badroulbadour had been taken. It is likely that he flew there on a magic carpet. As you probably know magic carpets have amazing powers that make you fly when you sit on them and say the magic words.

    Write a story called "**The Magic Carpet**". Describe how you discover the carpet and its magical powers, and the adventures you have.

    OR

2. In the last paragraph of the story we read that all the family were happily reunited in the palace. During each year there are often times when our families get together for a special event or celebration.

    Write a story called "**An Important Family Occasion**". Tell about what happened and also write about anything that you had to do as a part of the occasion.

- Remember that the examiners are looking to see if you have included speech correctly punctuated, feelings (of yourself or your characters) and good description.

- Remember to check your grammar, spelling and punctuation carefully.

- Write on lined paper.

....

....

....

....

....

....

....

....

....

....

....

....

....

....

....

....

....

....

....

....

....

....

....

....

T u t o r M a s t e r S e r v i c e s

ENGLISH
Comprehension

Standard Introductory
Paper 2B
40 minutes

Read the following carefully:

1. This paper is in two parts – a comprehension and a composition (story). You should spend about half an hour on each part.

2. Start this test when you are told to do so.

3. You should read the passage and then answer the questions about it. It is a good idea to look back at the passage to check your answers as many times as you want.

4. You should aim to finish all the questions.

5. Work as quickly and as carefully as you can.

6. You will have an extra 10 minutes reading time, 30 minutes to do the comprehension and 30 minutes for the composition.

Text © David Malindine

The right of David Malindine to be identified as author of this work has been asserted by him in accordance with the Copyright, Designs and Patents Act 1988.

Copyright © Tutor Master Services, 2015

Published by:

Tutor Master Services, 61 Ashness Gardens, Greenford, Middlesex UB6 0RW.

ISBN: 978-0-9555909-8-6

Read the passage below and answer the following questions carefully. It is a good idea to go back and check the passage to find your answers. Write your answers neatly on the answer sheet.

Androcles and the Lion

In Roman times, many hundreds of years of ago, lived a slave called Androcles. Desperate for his freedom, Androcles escaped from his master and fled to the forest...

With the hot sun beating down on his back, legs aching and heart pumping Androcles eventually reached the forest. He knew he would be safe here and hoped he would be able to survive if he were able to avoid wild animals and find enough roots and berries to eat. As a runaway slave he knew he would be executed if caught.

As Androcles peered around him, anxiously looking for pursuers, he felt the first splash of raindrops on his skin. It would soon be getting dark and he knew he needed to find shelter for the night. Through a gap in the trees Androcles spotted the opening of a cave in the hillside and he decided it would be an ideal place to spend the night.

Moving cautiously, lest a sound should alert those searching for him, Androcles made his way hesitantly towards the gaping mouth of the cave. When he reached the sanctuary of the opening he stepped inside and breathed a deep sigh of relief as he knew now he would be safe. He looked around, eyes searching in the gloom for a place to rest. Suddenly, as his sight became accustomed to the half-light he noticed the unmistakable outline of a great beast... a lion!

With his heart pounding with fear, Androcles prayed that the lion had already eaten and would not want to devour him where he stood. Androcles began to back out of the cave when suddenly the lion raised its great head and groaned and moaned, sorrowfully, or so Androcles thought.

Slowly, he retraced his steps and as he neared the lion it put out its paw. Androcles saw immediately that it was all swollen and bleeding. Androcles could see a huge thorn had embedded itself in the lion's paw which was causing all the pain. Speaking quietly and reassuringly to the suffering animal, Androcles gently pulled out the thorn and using some cloth torn from the hem of his tunic, cleaned and bound up the wound. The lion licked the hand of Androcles appreciatively and then shuddered, groaned, sighed and fell asleep. Exhausted after his ordeal, Androcles too fell into a deep sleep.

For the next few weeks, Androcles and the lion lived together in the large cave. The lion quickly recovered from its injury and was able to hunt, bringing Androcles fresh meat each day. Androcles regained his strength and soon was able to hunt and gather food, together with his new friend.

Whilst out collecting water on his own one day, Androcles was startled. "Stand still!" ordered a savage voice, "we know who you are and there's a big reward for runaway slaves, you're coming with us."

40 Androcles was captured and he knew there was no escape. Without delay Androcles was taken back to the city where he thought sadly about his friend, the lion, knowing they would never meet again.

Androcles was brought before the Roman Emperor in court and there he was sentenced to death. Confined in a small stone cell beneath the great
45 arena Androcles awaited his execution.

On the appointed day, Androcles was led out into the arena. Jeering crowds thronged the terraces roaring their approval as a great lion was loosed. The lion, hungry, as it had not been fed for several days, bounded towards the helpless man. Roaring ravenously, the lion prepared to devour its victim.

50 Androcles knew he was finished and prepared for the onslaught of the first slashing blow and searing pain.

However, the expected wait for slashing claws and tearing jaws did not come. Instead, Androcles felt the tongue of the lion as it washed his face and licked him like a friendly dog. The lion recognised Androcles as his
55 friend from the forest and nuzzled him as the man who had so gently cared for him.

The crowd was instantly silenced, and the Emperor astonished by what he had witnessed. He summoned Androcles to him, who told him the whole story.

60 "This man is pardoned," announced the Emperor, "and is to be set free. Such kindness and gratitude between fierce enemies should be highly regarded. This is the lion, a man's friend; this is the man, a lion's doctor."

At this Androcles was set free and the lion let loose to return to his native forest.

ANSWER SECTION

PLEASE WRITE YOUR FULL NAME HERE:

_____

MARKS

1. Androcles is suffering as he strives to make his escape. Write down three verbs from the sentence (line 3) that tell us this.

    3

    1) ....

    2) ....

    3) ....

2. In paragraph 2 (lines 3 - 7), we are told that Androcles is a runaway slave seeking safety in a forest. Write down two things he will need to do in order to survive.

    2

    1) ....

    2) ....

3. "As Androcles peered around him, anxiously looking for pursuers" (line 8), give the part of speech of the words in the table. Choose from the box below:

    5

verb; adverb; pronoun; proper noun; preposition

Word	Part of speech
Androcles	
peered	
around	
him	
anxiously	

4. In your own words explain why Androcles is both feeling worried and also relieved in paragraph 3 (lines 8 - 12).

4

....

....

....

....

....

5. Write down the two adverbs used in paragraph 4 (lines 13 - 19) to describe how Androcles is nervous as he moves in the direction of the cave.

2

1) ....   2) ....

6. The following is a list of events which happen in paragraph 4 (lines 13 - 19). They have been mixed up. You must try to put them back in order by writing numbers 1 - 5 against each one. The last one has been done for you.

5

Androcles stepped into the cave.   ....

He saw the lion.   **6** ....

He approached the cave.   ....

Androcles moved cautiously.   ....

He breathed a sigh of relief.   ....

He looked around.   ....

7. Put a ring around the word which is closest in meaning to the word "devour" (line 21) as it is used in the passage.

2

      bite   consume   chase   nibble

8. What was causing the lion to moan sorrowfully (line 23)?

3

....

....

....

....

9. Androcles carried out four actions to help the lion in paragraph 6 (lines 24 - 32). What were they?

4

1)...

....

2)...

....

3)...

....

4)...

....

10. How does paragraph 7 (lines 33 - 36) tell us that Androcles and the lion became close friends?

3

....

....

....

....

....

....

11. Put a ring around the word which is closest in meaning to the word "confined" (line 44) as it is used in the passage.

2

      imprisoned   released   liberated   freed

12. From paragraph 12 (lines 50 - 51) copy down two phrases that tell us that Androcles expected his death to be painful.

4

1)...

2)...

13. Write down an example of alliteration found in paragraph 11 (lines 46 - 49).   **3**

....

14. Re-read paragraphs 11 - 14 (lines 46 - 59), then explain in your own words why "the crowd was instantly silenced" and the "Emperor astonished" by what they had witnessed.   **3**

....

....

....

....

....

....

....

....

....

15. Find and copy down a phrase from the passage that means the same as "mocking spectators crowded the steps bawling their agreement".   **3**

....

....

....

....

16. Put a ring around the word that does not mean the same as "pardoned" (line 60).   **2**

    forgiven   absolved   reprieved   guilty

TOTAL MARKS =   **50**

END OF QUESTIONS ON PART ONE

Tutor *Master* *Services*

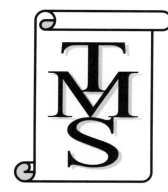

ENGLISH
Composition/Essay

30 minutes
Total Marks: 50

Choose one of these to write

1. Androcles and the Lion is a story about an unusual friendship that develops between a man and a lion. Often friendships do not begin like this!

   Write a story called "**My First Best Friend**" where you write about the first best friend you ever had, or about a friend that you have known for a long time. Write about how and where you met, describe your friend's appearance, character and personality, tell about some things you do together and also say what are the qualities that make the friendship strong.

   OR

2. Imagine you are a reporter for a local newspaper. Soon after Androcles is set free your editor asks you to write a report of this amazing story. Use information from the passage, plus your imagination to tell the story.

   You should include:
   a) How the story began with Androcles, a runaway slave seeking safety.
   b) How Androcles encountered the lion and the development of their friendship.
   c) The capture of Androcles, the unusual events that took place in the arena and the release of Androcles. Include too, an interview with Androcles where he explains his feelings about the events.

   Use the headline "**Androcles Alive! Arena Audience Astonished!**".

- Remember that the examiners are looking to see if you have included speech correctly punctuated, feelings (of yourself or your characters) and good description.

- Remember to check your grammar, spelling and punctuation carefully.

- Write on lined paper.

....

....

....

....

....

....

....

....

....

....

....

....

....

....

....

....

....

....

....

....

....

....

....

....

....

....

....

....

....

....

....

....

....

....

....

....

....

....

....

....

....

....

....

....

....

....

....

....

....

....

....

....

....

....

....

....

....

....

....

....

....

....

....

....

....

....

....

....

TutorMasterServices

ENGLISH
Comprehension

Standard Introductory
Paper 2C

40 minutes

Read the following carefully:

1. This paper is in two parts – a comprehension and a composition (story). You should spend about half an hour on each part.

2. Start this test when you are told to do so.

3. You should read the passage and then answer the questions about it. It is a good idea to look back at the passage to check your answers as many times as you want.

4. You should aim to finish all the questions.

5. Work as quickly and as carefully as you can.

6. You will have an extra 10 minutes reading time, 30 minutes to do the comprehension and 30 minutes for the composition.

Text © David Malindine

The right of David Malindine to be identified as author of this work has been asserted by him in accordance with the Copyright, Designs and Patents Act 1988.

Copyright © Tutor Master Services, 2015

Published by:

Tutor Master Services, 61 Ashness Gardens, Greenford, Middlesex UB6 0RW.

ISBN: 978-0-9555909-8-6

Read the passage below and answer the following questions carefully. It is a good idea to go back and check the passage to find your answers. Write your answers neatly on the answer sheet.

The Myth of Daedalus and Icarus

The tale of Daedalus (Day-da-lus) and Icarus (Ick-ar-us) goes back thousands of years to the time of ancient Greece. It is a myth, a made up story which the ancient Greek writers are famous for.

In ancient Greece there once lived a man named Daedalus. He lived and
5   worked in the great city of Athens where he gained fame and fortune as a skilled and talented architect, sculptor and inventor who produced many fine works. Working alongside Daedalus and learning his trade was his nephew and apprentice Talus who seemed destined to become as great a workman as his uncle.

10 One day Talus came to Daedalus and showed him an invention he had developed. He had made a saw after watching how the teeth of a snake had used its jaws to cut. Surprisingly Daedalus was immediately jealous of Talus and in a fit of anger threw him off a tall building to his death. For this crime Daedalus was punished by the King of Greece and he was sent away
15 to the island of Crete to work for King Minos.

While living on Crete, Daedalus met and married a beautiful woman and together they had a son named Icarus.

Now King Minos of Crete had a big problem. Living on the island was a fearsome and terrible monster known as the Minatour which had the head
20 of a bull and the body of a man. He decided to imprison the creature in the Labyrinth, a series of underground caves. To build the caves King Minos instructed Daedalus to design and construct them, which he did.

Then one day the King of Athens – Theseus – arrived in Crete determined to kill the dreaded Minotaur, but he faced the problem of trying to find, kill the
25 monster and then escape from the Labyrinth. King Minos had a daughter named Ariadne and she was determined to help Theseus in his quest to kill the Minotaur. She went to Daedalus and asked him to reveal to her the mystery of the Labyrinth. Daedalus instructed her and then, because she was in love with Theseus, she went to him to advise him. Ariadne provided
30 Theseus with a ball of string which he used to help guide himself back out of the caves once he had killed the Minotaur.

When King Minos found out what Daedalus had done he was so enraged that he imprisoned Daedalus in a tall tower, all alone with Icarus, his young son.

35 Now Daedalus and Icarus did not like being prisoners and were determined to escape. Daedalus watched the birds flying over the sea towards Greece and thought to himself, "How free they are, if they can fly away, why can't we?" Daedalus and Icarus decided to use their skills to make wings to be able to fly to freedom.

40 Working secretly they used wax and string to fasten feathers to reeds of varying lengths. They made the wings very large so that they could support the heavy weight of a person and they put straps on them so that they could be attached to their arms. The wings were curved to imitate the curves of the birds' wings.

45 When their wings were ready, Daedalus gave his son a strict warning for when he was flying: if he flew too near to the sea his wings may dampen, get wet and he may fall in and be drowned, but if he flew too high in the sky, the heat of the sun would melt the wax on his wings and he would fall. Icarus promised to be careful.

50 So they set off, flying for freedom. At first everything went well, but the young Icarus, overwhelmed by the thrill of flying, began to try to do tricks and stunts. His father, concerned for his safety, ordered him to behave but Icarus was exhilarated by the sense of freedom and having too much fun, so he ignored his father's warning. Higher and higher he rose; upwards,
55 upwards and nearer the sun, when suddenly the heat from the bright sunlight melted the wax in his wings. Icarus kept flapping and flapping his wings until he had no feathers left and he was only flapping his bare arms. Down, down, down he fell into the sea where he drowned.

Daedalus looked down to see feathers floating in the water and realised
60 what had happened. Daedalus escaped to the island of Sicily but only after he had buried his son on a tiny island which nowadays is called Icaria. The sea around this island into which Icarus had plunged is named the Icarian sea to this very day.

ANSWER SECTION

PLEASE WRITE YOUR FULL NAME HERE:

_____

MARKS

1. Write down the names of the two characters mentioned in the second paragraph (lines 4 - 9).

   2

   1) ……………………………………………………………………………

   2) ……………………………………………………………………………

2. Daedalus was skilled in three ways, write them down

   3

   1) as an ……………………………………………………………………

   2) as a ……………………………………………………………………

   3) as an ……………………………………………………………………

3. In paragraph 3 (lines 10 - 15) both Talus and Daedalus experienced different feelings. Complete the table to show their different feelings. Choose **three** words from the box below:

   3

pride; sadness; love; envy; calmness; rage

Character	Feelings
Daedalus	1) ……………………………………………… 2) ………………………………………………
Talus	1) ………………………………………………

4. Complete the table below to show the relationships between the characters mentioned in this story. Choose names from the box below.

6

> Daedalus; Minos; daughter of Minos; Theseus;
> nephew of Daedalus; Theseus

Name	Relationship
	Father of Icarus
Talus	
	King of Crete
	King of Athens
Ariadne	
	Boyfriend of Ariadne

5. In your own words explain what the Labyrinth was and why it was needed.

3

....

....

....

....

....

....

6. Explain why you think King Minos particularly chose Daedalus to design and construct the Labyrinth.

3

....

....

....

....

....

7. In paragraph 6 (lines 23 - 31) Theseus arrived in Crete determined to kill the Minotaur. Name the three problems he faced:

3

1)...

....

2)...

....

3)...

....

8. Explain what you think was "the mystery of the Labyrinth" (lines 27 -28).

2

....

....

....

....

....

9. How did Ariadne assist Theseus to solve "the mystery of the Labyrinth"?

4

....

....

....

....

....

10. How did watching birds inspire Daedalus and Icarus to plan their escape?

2

....

....

....

....

11. In paragraph 9 (lines 40 - 44) Daedalus and Icarus made their wings. Write down the three particular things they **<u>designed</u>** to make the wings work properly.

3

1)...

....

2)...

....

3)...

....

12. Flying with homemade wings could cause problems for Icarus. Explain what might happen if he flew too high or too low.

4

Too high ....

....

....

....

Too low ....

....

....

....

13. Put a ring around the word which is closest in meaning to the word "destined" (line 8) as it is used in the passage.

2

      usual   remotely   certain   unlikely

14. Put a ring around the word which is closest in meaning to the word "enraged" (line 32) as it is used in the passage.

2

      calm   frustrated   determined   infuriated

15. Put a ring around the word which is closest in meaning to the word "imitate" (line 43) as it is used in the passage.

2

      irritate   copy   dictate   regulate

16. Find and copy down from the passage words or phrases that mean the same as:

a) Daedalus achieved celebrity status and riches. **2**

Words or phrase …………………………………………………………………

…………………………………………………………………………………

…………………………………………………………………………………

b) Daedalus and Icarus were winging their way to liberty. **2**

Words or phrase …………………………………………………………………

…………………………………………………………………………………

…………………………………………………………………………………

c) Icarus was overcome by the excitement of being airborne. **2**

Words or phrase …………………………………………………………………

…………………………………………………………………………………

…………………………………………………………………………………

TOTAL MARKS = 50

END OF QUESTIONS ON PART ONE

Tutor Master Services

ENGLISH
Composition/Essay

30 minutes
Total Marks: 50

Choose one of these to write

1. In the story you have read, Daedalus and Icarus use their imagination and skills to make large, curved wings that they can strap on and fly in freedom.

    Write a story called "**Things I Have Made**" where you tell about something or some things you have made. These could be models made from a kit, or things you have made in the house or garden or at school, a holiday club or an activities centre.

    Write about planning, organising materials, the process of making and what you did with the finished item.

    OR

2. Use your imagination to write out the speech conversation that takes place between Daedalus and Icarus as they plan to design and make their wings. Include too the warnings that Daedalus gave to Icarus and his response.

    Use the title "**Speech Conversation between Icarus and Daedalus**".

*   Remember that the examiners are looking to see if you have included speech correctly punctuated, feelings (of yourself or your characters) and good description.

*   Remember to check your grammar, spelling and punctuation carefully.

*   Write on lined paper.

....

....

....

....

....

....

....

....

....

....

....

....

....

....

....

....

....

....

....

....

....

....

....

....

....

....

....

....

....

....

....

....

....

....

....

....

....

....

....

....

....

....

....

....

....

....

....

....

....

....

....

....

....

....

....

....

....

....

....

....

....

....

....

....

....

....

....

....

TutorMasterServices

ENGLISH
Comprehension
Standard Introductory
Paper 2D
40 minutes

Read the following carefully:

1. This paper is in two parts – a comprehension and a composition (story). You should spend about half an hour on each part.

2. Start this test when you are told to do so.

3. You should read the passage and then answer the questions about it. It is a good idea to look back at the passage to check your answers as many times as you want.

4. You should aim to finish all the questions.

5. Work as quickly and as carefully as you can.

6. You will have an extra 10 minutes reading time, 30 minutes to do the comprehension and 30 minutes for the composition.

Text © David Malindine

The right of David Malindine to be identified as author of this work has been asserted by him in accordance with the Copyright, Designs and Patents Act 1988.

Copyright © Tutor Master Services, 2015

Published by:

Tutor Master Services, 61 Ashness Gardens, Greenford, Middlesex UB6 0RW.

ISBN: 978-0-9555909-8-6

Read the passage below and answer the following questions carefully. It is a good idea to go back and check the passage to find your answers. Write your answers neatly on the answer sheet.

The Wild Wood

In this extract from 'The Wind in the Willows', Mole decides to pay a visit to Mr Badger who lives deep in the Wild Wood.

It was a cold still afternoon when Mole slipped out of his warm snug parlour to visit Mr Badger in the Wild Wood. Now that the leafy summer was over,
5   the countryside lay undecorated, hard and stripped of its finery. With great cheerfulness of spirit, Mole pushed on towards the Wild Wood which lay before him low and threatening like a black reef in some still southern sea.

There was nothing to alarm him at first. Twigs crackled under his feet, logs tripped him up, trees took on ugly crouching shapes that seemed to
10   approach him on every side.

Everything was very still now. The light was fading as dusk advanced on him steadily, rapidly, gathering in behind and before; the light seemed to be draining away like flood-water. Mole began to feel frightened.

Then the faces began.

15   It was over his shoulder and indistinctly that he first thought he saw a face: a little wedge-shaped face, looking out at him from a hole. When he turned and confronted it, the thing had vanished.

He quickened his pace, telling himself cheerfully not to begin imagining things, or there would simply be no end of it. He passed another hole,
20   and another, and another, and then – yes! – no! – yes! Certainly a little narrow face, with hard eyes, had flashed up for an instant from a hole and was gone. Mole hesitated – braced himself up for an effort and strode on. Then suddenly, every hole, far and near, and there were hundreds of them, seemed to possess its face, coming and going rapidly, all fixing on
25   him glances of malice and hatred: all hard-eyed and evil and sharp.

If only he could get away from the holes in the banks, he thought, there would be no more faces. He swung off the path and plunged into the untrodden places of the wood.

Then the whistling began.

30   Very faint and shrill it was, and far behind him, when first he heard it; but somehow it made him hurry forward. Then, still very faint and shrill it sounded far ahead of him and made him hesitate and want to go back. As he halted in indecision it broke out on either side. They were up and alert and ready, evidently, whoever they were! And he – he was alone, and
35   unarmed, and far from any help and the night was closing in.

Then the pattering began.

He thought it was only falling leaves at first, so slight and delicate was the

40 sound of it. Then as the sound grew it took a regular rhythm and he knew it for nothing else but the pat-pat-pat of tiny feet, still a long way off. Was it in front or behind? It seemed to be first one, then the other, then both. It grew and it multiplied, till from every quarter as he listened anxiously, leaning this way and that, it seemed to be closing in on him. As he stood still to hearken, a rabbit came running hard towards him through the trees. He waited, expecting it to slacken pace, or to swerve from him into a different 45 course. Instead the animal almost brushed him as it dashed past, his face set and hard, his eyes staring. "Get out of this, you fool, get out!" Mole heard him mutter as he swung round a tree stump and disappeared down a friendly burrow.

50 Meanwhile, Rat had discovered Mole was not at home. He saw his footprints outside leading to the Wild Wood. Seizing a stout stick, he set out at a smart pace to track him. At last he found Mole huddled in the shelter of an old beech tree, trembling all over and so glad his friend had come.

From *The Wind in the Willows* by Kenneth Grahame

ANSWER SECTION

PLEASE WRITE YOUR FULL NAME HERE:

_____

MARKS

1. Three characters are mentioned in the story. Write down their names.   **3**

   Character one ....

   Character two ....

   Character three ....

2. What time of day and what season of the year was it when Mole set out on his walk?   **2**

   Time of day ....

   Season ....

3. Put a ring around the word that best describes how Mole was feeling as he set out.   **2**

   light-hearted   sad   fearful   apprehensive

4. 'the Wild Wood which lay before him low and threatening like a black reef in some still southern sea' (lines 6 - 7). What name do we give to this type of comparison?   **2**

   ....

5. In paragraphs 3 and 4 (lines 8 - 13) Mole begins to get scared. Write down three things that frightened him.   **3**

   1) ....

   ....

   2) ....

   ....

   3) ....

   ....

6. There is a simile in paragraph 4, copy it out accurately.

2

....

....

....

....

7. How many 'faces' does Mole see?

2

....

....

....

8. Where are faces appearing from?

2

....

....

....

9. The faces have expressions of hostility to Mole. From paragraph 7 (lines 18 - 25) pick out five words that tell us this.

5

1) ....   4) ....

2) ....   5) ....

3) ....

10. What does Mole do to escape the faces?

3

....

....

....

....

11. In paragraph 10 (lines 30 - 35) Mole reacts to the whistling by changing his movements in three different ways. Write them out.

    1)...

    2)...

    3)...

3

12. Paragraph 10 (lines 30 - 35) ends with Mole standing stock-still and very scared. Pick out and write down four reasons why he feels like this.

    1)...

    2)...

    3)...

    4)...

4

13. What did the 'pattering' sound like to Mole?

    ....

    ....

    ....

    ....

2

14. The following is a list of events which happen in paragraph 12 (lines 37 - 48). They have been mixed up. You must try to put them back in order by writing numbers 1 - 5 against each one. The last one has been done for you.

The rabbit disappeared   .   **6** ....

The rabbit warned Mole.   ....

A rabbit ran towards Mole.   ....

The pattering made a steady beat.   ....

Mole waited.   ....

Mole listened anxiously.   ....

5

15. Which friend eventually found Mole?　　　　　　　　　　　　　　　　**2**

....

....

16. Find and copy down from paragraph 12 (lines 37 - 48) words or phrases that
mean the same as;

a) The pattering sound was barely audible.　　　　　　　　　　　　　**2**

Words or phrase ....

....

....

b) The pattering sound came from all directions.　　　　　　　　　　**2**

Words or phrase ....

....

....

c) Mole stood still to listen　　　　　　　　　　　　　　　　　　　**2**

Words or phrase ....

....

....

d) slow down　　　　　　　　　　　　　　　　　　　　　　　　　**2**

Words or phrase ....

....

....

TOTAL MARKS =　　**50**

END OF QUESTIONS ON PART ONE

Tutor Master Services

ENGLISH
Composition/Essay

30 minutes
Total Marks: 50

Choose one of these to write

1. This story has a happy ending when Rat finds Mole and is a case of "All's well that ends well!" It is an example of good news.

   From time to time we all hear or receive good news. In this story you will write about a time when you received some good news. You will need to say what the good news was, how you received it and you will need to tell the reader your feelings about the news. Use the title "**Good News**".

   OR

2. Imagine that when Mole gets home he decides to write a letter to Badger to tell him the reasons why he did not arrive at his house. Use your imagination to pretend you are Mole and explain:

   a) How you set off with eager anticipation to see your old friend.

   b) How your feelings changed as your journey became steadily more difficult and unpleasant.

   c) Being discovered at last by Rat and how you felt when you realised he had found you.

   Use the title "**My Letter to Mr Badger**".

- Remember that the examiners are looking to see if you have included speech correctly punctuated, feelings (of yourself or your characters) and good description.

- Remember to check your grammar, spelling and punctuation carefully.

- Write on lined paper.

....

....

....

....

....

....

....

....

....

....

....

....

....

....

....

....

....

....

....

....

....

....

TutorMasterServices

ENGLISH
Comprehension
Standard Introductory
Paper 2E
40 minutes

Read the following carefully:

1. This paper is in two parts – a comprehension and a composition (story). You should spend about half an hour on each part.

2. Start this test when you are told to do so.

3. You should read the passage and then answer the questions about it. It is a good idea to look back at the passage to check your answers as many times as you want.

4. You should aim to finish all the questions.

5. Work as quickly and as carefully as you can.

6. You will have an extra 10 minutes reading time, 30 minutes to do the comprehension and 30 minutes for the composition.

Text © David Malindine

The right of David Malindine to be identified as author of this work has been asserted by him in accordance with the Copyright, Designs and Patents Act 1988.

Copyright © Tutor Master Services, 2015

Published by:

Tutor Master Services, 61 Ashness Gardens, Greenford, Middlesex UB6 0RW.

ISBN: 978-0-9555909-8-6

Read the passage below and answer the following questions carefully. It is a good idea to go back and check the passage to find your answers. Write your answers neatly on the answer sheet.

The Fire

This extract is from the story of 'Black Beauty'. It tells of the life, many years ago, of a young male horse – a colt. In this story the narrator is the horse.

Later on in the evening, a traveller's horse was brought in by a second ostler, and whilst he was cleaning him a young man with a pipe in his mouth
5   lounged into the stable to gossip.

"I say, Towler," said the ostler, "just run up the ladder into the loft and bring down some hay into this horse's rack, will you? Only first lay down your pipe."

"All right," said the other, and he went up through the trap door. I heard
10   him step across the floor overhead and put down the hay. James came in to look at us the last thing, and the door was locked.

I cannot say how long I had slept, nor what time in the night it was, but I woke up feeling very uncomfortable, though I hardly knew why. I got up; the air seemed all thick and choking. I heard Ginger coughing, and one of
15   the other horses moved about restlessly. It was quite dark, and I could see nothing; but the stable was full of smoke, and I hardly knew how to breathe.

The trap door had been left open, and I thought that was the place from which the smoke came. I listened and heard a soft, rushing sort of noise, and a low crackling and snapping. I did not know what it was, but there
20   was something in the sound so strange that it made me tremble all over. The other horses were now all awake; some were pulling at their halters, others were stamping.

At last I heard steps outside, and the ostler who had put up the traveller's horse burst into the stable with a lantern, and began to untie the horses, and
25   try to lead them out; but he seemed in such a hurry, and was so frightened himself, that he frightened me still more. The first horse would not go with him; he tried the second and third, but they too would not stir. He came to me next and tried to drag me out of the stall by force; of course that was no use. He tried us all by turns and then left the stable.

30   No doubt we were very foolish, but danger seemed to be all round; there was nobody whom we knew to trust in, and all was strange and uncertain. The fresh air that had come in through the open door made it easier to breathe, but the rushing sound overhead grew louder, and as I looked upward, through the bars of my empty rack, I saw a red light flickering on
35   the wall. Then I heard a cry of 'Fire!' outside, and the old ostler came quietly and quickly in. He got one horse out, and went to another; but the flames were playing round the trap door, and the roaring overhead was dreadful.

The next thing I heard was James's voice, quiet and cheery, as it always was.

*ostler = someone employed in a stable to take care of the horses

"Come, my beauties, it is time for us to be off, so wake up and come along."
I stood nearest the door, so he came to me first, patting me as he came in.

"Come, Beauty, on with your bridle, my boy, we'll soon be out of this smother." It was on in no time; then he took the scarf off his neck, and tied it lightly over my eyes, and, patting and coaxing, he led me out of the stable. Safe in the yard, he slipped the scarf off my eyes, and shouted, "Here somebody! Take this horse while I go back for the other."

A tall, broad man stepped forward and took me, and James darted back into the stable. I set up a shrill whinny as I saw him go. Ginger told me afterwards that whinny was the best thing I could have done for her, for had she not heard me outside, she would never have had courage to come out.

There was much confusion in the yard; the horses were being got out of other stables, and the carriages and gigs were being pulled out of houses and sheds, lest the flames should spread further. On the other side of the yard windows were thrown open, and people were shouting all sorts of things; but I kept my eye fixed on the stable door, where the smoke poured out thicker than ever, and I could see flashes of red light.

Presently, I heard above all the stir and din a loud, clear voice, which I knew was master's:-

"James Howard! James Howard! Are you there?" There was no answer, but I heard a crash of something falling in the stable, and the next moment I gave a loud, joyful neigh, for I saw James coming through the smoke, leading Ginger with him; she was coughing violently and he was not able to speak.

"My brave lad!" said master, laying his hand on his shoulder. "Are you hurt?"

James shook his head for he could not speak yet.

"Ay," said the big man who held me, "he is a brave lad, and no mistake."

"And now," said master, "when you have got your breath, James, we'll get out of this place as quickly as we can."

We were moving towards the entry when from the Market Place there came a sound of galloping feet and loud rumbling wheels.

"Tis the fire engine! The fire engine!" shouted two or three voices. "Stand back, make way!" And clattering and thundering over the stones two horses dashed into the yard with the heavy engine behind them. The firemen leaped to the ground; there was no need to ask where the fire was – it was torching up in a great blaze from the roof.

From _Black Beauty_ by Anna Sewell

ANSWER SECTION

PLEASE WRITE YOUR FULL NAME HERE:

_____

MARKS

1. This story is being narrated by one of the following. Put a ring around the correct name.   **2**

    a traveller   Towler   James   a horse

2. At what time of day does this story take place?   **2**

    ....

3. Find and copy down a phrase from paragraph 2 (lines 3 - 5) that is closest in meaning to "dawdled into the barn for a chat".   **2**

    ....

    ....

4. Who or what is Ginger, the name mentioned in line 14?   **2**

    ....

5. In paragraph 5 (lines 12 - 16), we are told that "the stable was full of smoke". Write down four effects that the **smoke** had on the horses.   **4**

    a) ....

    b) ....

    c) ....

    d) ....

6. Find and copy down a sentence from paragraph 6 (lines 17 - 22) that tells us that the fire is taking hold.   **2**

    ....

    ....

    ....

7. From paragraph 6 (lines 17 - 22) choose and write down four effects that the **fire**   **4**
   was having on the horses.

   a) ....

   b) ....

   c) ....

   d) ....

8. In lines 24 and 25 the ostler attempts to save the horses. Write down three   **3**
   phrases that tell us this.

   a) ....

   b) ....

   c) ....

9. Explain why the ostler was unsuccessful in his attempts to lead the horses to   **3**
   safety.

   ....

   ....

   ....

   ....

10. In paragraph 8 (lines 30 - 37) pick out two adverbs that tell us that the old ostler   **2**
    had a more effective approach to the horses.

    1) ....

    2) ....

11. How is James's voice described in paragraph 9 and say what effect this is likely   **4**
    to have on the horses.

   ....

   ....

   ....

   ....

12. The following is a list of things that happen in the paragraph 10 (lines 41 - 45). **7**
They have been mixed up. You must try to put them back in order by writing
numbers 1 - 8 against each one. The last one has been done for you.

James took off his scarf. ………

James patted the horse. ………

James led the horse out of the stable. ………

James shouted. **8**
………

James coaxed the horse. ………

James tied the scarf over the horse's eyes. ………

James slipped the scarf off the horse's eyes. ………

James put on the bridle. ………

13. Put a ring around the word which is closest in meaning to the word "darted" **2**
(line 46) as it is used in the passage.

saentered   strolled   dashed   ambled

14. Explain how the "shrill whinny" made by Black Beauty was the best thing he **3**
could have done for Ginger.

....

....

....

....

....

15. In lines 70 - 71, we are told "there came a sound of galloping feet and loud **2**
rumbling wheels". What was making these sounds?

....

....

16. Find and copy down from the passage words or phrases that mean the same as:

a) He wanted to move us out of the stable one by one.

2

Words or phrase …………………………………………………………………

…………………………………………………………………………………

…………………………………………………………………………………

b) Fire was flickering round the entrance hatch.

2

Words or phrase …………………………………………………………………

…………………………………………………………………………………

…………………………………………………………………………………

c) Above all the hullabaloo and racket

2

Words or phrase …………………………………………………………………

…………………………………………………………………………………

…………………………………………………………………………………

TOTAL MARKS =   **50**

END OF QUESTIONS ON PART ONE

T u t o r *M a s t e r* *S e r v i c e s*

ENGLISH
Composition/Essay

30 minutes
Total Marks: 50

Choose one of these to write

1. This story is unusual as the narrator (story teller) is a horse. The events are described from the horse's point of view. Your task is to choose an animal - it can be a wild animal, a bird or a fish or perhaps a pet - and to use your imagination to write a story based on one day and told through the eyes of the animal, bird, fish, or pet. (Remember to use the personal pronoun 'I' as you write!)

   Use the title "**A Day in the Life of a ...**".

   OR

2. Use your imagination to write out the speech conversation that takes place between James and the Master after they have got out of the blazing stables and to a place of safety. The Master will want to know about the possible causes of the fire and the actions James took to save the horses, while James will be keen to explain all he knows.

   Use the title "**Speech Conversation between James and the Master**".

- Remember that the examiners are looking to see if you have included speech correctly punctuated, feelings (of yourself or your characters) and good description.

- Remember to check your grammar, spelling and punctuation carefully.

- Write on lined paper.

....
....
....
....
....
....
....
....
....
....
....
....
....
....
....
....
....
....
....
....
....
....
....

Tutor Master Services

ENGLISH
Comprehension

Answers and Marking Schemes
for
Standard Introductory
Papers 1 – 5
and
Compositions

www.tutormaster-services.co.uk

Answers to Paper 2A

Question number	Answer	Mark	Parent's notes and additional comments
1	lazy lad, idle son, impoverished ne'er-do-well	3	In any order
2	(see table below)	6	
3	Aladdin and his mother were surprised because they had always thought that Uncle Mustafa had died.	2	
4	Aladdin and his uncle set off on a long journey because they wanted to buy stock to begin their trading venture/set up young Aladdin as a merchant	3	
5	Uncle Mustafa pulls on the ring. …4… Uncle Mustafa promised Aladdin gread wealth. …6… Uncle Mustafa lit a fire. …1… Steps were revealed. …5… Uncle Mustafa produced some magic powder. …2… A stone slab was revealed. …3…	5	No mark given for **1** as this was given in the question.
6	was eventually won over (by his uncle)	2	
7	Aladdin does not hand over the lamp he has found in the cave to his uncle as he was not yet safely out of the cave.	3	
8	Mustafa became angry and spoke some magic words which made the stone slab slam shut trapping Aladdin in the cave.	3	
9	The genie of the ring helped Aladdin to escape from the cave and took him home to his mother. The genie of the lamp appears after Aladdin rubs their old lamp and with his help Aladdin and his mother became rich and successful by selling silverware that the genie produces magically for them. The genie of the lamp also helps Aladdin and his princess to move into a magnificent palace.	3	Any 1 mark for each correct point made.
10	new lamps for old	3	line 45

Question 2 table:

Name	Relationship
Qaseem	Aladdin's father
Aladdin	**Mustafa's nephew**
Uncle Mustafa	**magician**
Sultan	Aladdin's father-in-law
Prince Badroulbadour	**Aladdin's wife**
Uncle Mustafa	wicked uncle

Question number	Answer	Mark	Parent's notes and additional comments
	English Comprehension Standard Introductory Set Two Answers		
11	sad, anxious, alone	3	
12	shameful	2	
13	faithful	2	
14	impending	2	
15a	had constantly refused him his wish	2	lines 56 - 57
15b	hatched a cunning plan	2	lines 58 - 59
15c	bedazzled by her beauty and charms	2	line 63
16a	In a land far away (to the East)	1	line 1
16b	and they all lived happily ever after	1	line 71

Answers to Paper 2B

Question number	Answer	Mark	Parent's notes and additional comments
1	beating, aching, pumping	3	In any order
2	avoid wild animals, find enough roots and berries to eat	2	In any order
3	<table><tr><td>Word</td><td>Parts of Speech</td></tr><tr><td>Androcles</td><td>proper noun</td></tr><tr><td>peered</td><td>verb</td></tr><tr><td>around</td><td>preposition</td></tr><tr><td>him</td><td>pronoun</td></tr><tr><td>anxiously</td><td>adverb</td></tr></table>	5	
4	Androcles is feeling worried because he is being chased, it is starting to rain, it will soon be getting dark and he needs shelter. Androcles is feeling relieved because he saw a cave in the hillside that he thought would be an ideal place to shelter for the night.	4	Use discretion to award marks for something similar. Encourage students to separate their answer into 2 parts.
5	cautiously, hesitantly	2	

Question number	Answer	Mark	Parent's notes and additional comments
6	Androcles stepped into the cave. …3… He saw the lion. …**6**… He approached the cave. …2… Androcles moved cautiously. …1… He breathed a sigh of relief. …4… He looked around. …5…	5	No mark given for **6** as this was given in the question.
7	consume	2	
8	A huge thorn had embedded itself in the lion's paw and it was causing pain.	3	
9	He spoke quietly and reassuringly. He pulled out the thorn. He cleaned the wound. He bound up the wound.	4	In any order
10	They lived together in the large cave. The lion hunted and brought food for Androcles to eat. Androcles became stronger so that they could go out hunting together. Soon they became close friends.	3	1 mark for each correct point made.
11	imprisoned	2	
12	slashing blow searing pain	4	
13	roaring ravenously or lion was loosed	3	
14	The crowd was silenced because instead of attacking Androcles and eating him up as they had expected, the lion seemed to greet Androcles as an old friend and treated him with care and affection. The Emperor was astonished as he had seen something so unusual he couldn't believe his eyes. He expected Androcles and the lion to be enemies, but instead they were friends.	3	Use discretion to award marks for something similar. Encourage students to separate their answer into 2 parts.
15	Jeering crowds thronged the terraces roaring their approval.	3	lines 46 - 47
16	guilty	2	

Answers to Paper 2C

Question number	Answer	Mark	Parent's notes and additional comments
1	Daedalus, Talus	2	
2	architect, sculptor, inventor	3	Answer can be in any order.
3	<table><tr><td>Daedalus</td><td>1) envy 2) rage</td></tr><tr><td>Talus</td><td>pride</td></tr></table>	3	Answer can be in any order.
4	<table><tr><th>Name</th><th>Relationship</th></tr><tr><td>**Daedalus**</td><td>Father of Icarus</td></tr><tr><td>Talus</td><td>**nephew of Daedalus**</td></tr><tr><td>**Minos**</td><td>King of Crete</td></tr><tr><td>**Theseus**</td><td>King of Athens</td></tr><tr><td>Ariadne</td><td>**daughter of Minos**</td></tr><tr><td>**Theseus**</td><td>boyfriend of Ariadne</td></tr></table>	6	
5	The Labyrinth was a series of underground caves designed and constructed by Daedalus. The Labyrinth was needed because King Minos had a problem with a terrible monster called the Minatour. He wanted to imprison the Minatour in the Labyrinth.	3	Use your discretion to award marks for something similar. Encourage students to give a 2 part answer to this 2 part question.
6	Daedalus had all the skills needed to design and construct the Labyrinth as he was skilled as an architect, sculptor and inventor,	3	
7	1) to find the Minatour 2) to kill the Minatour 3) to escape from the Labyrinth	3	Answer can be in any order.
8	The mystery of the Labyrinth was that the underground caves were confusing and complicated. It was very difficult/impossible to find your way out once you were inside.	2	
9	1) Ariadne asked Daedalus to explain to her how to get out of the Labyrinth once you were inside. 2) Ariadne gave Theseus a ball of string which he tied at the entrance and unravelled as he went in. To get back out he just followed the string.	4	Answer can be in any order. Use your discretion to award marks for something similar.

English Comprehension Standard Introductory Set Two Answers

Question number	Answer	Mark	Parent's notes and additional comments
10	They watched the birds flying freely and they thought that they could copy the birds by flying to freedom.	2	Use your discretion to award marks for something similar.
11	1) They made the wings very large. 2) They put straps on them. 3) They made the wings curved like bird's wings.	3	Answer can be in any order.
12	Too high: The heat of the sun would melt the wax on his wings and he would fall. Too low: He would be too near the sea so his wings would dampen, get wet and he may fall into the sea and be drowned.	4	Use your discretion to award marks for something similar.
13	certain	2	
14	infuriated	2	
15	copy	2	
16 a	he gained fame and fortune	2	line 5
16 b	Flying for freedom	2	line 50
16 c	overwhelmed by the thrill of flying	2	line 51

Answers to Paper 2D

Question number	Answer	Mark	Parent's notes and additional comments
1	Mole, Badger, Rat	3	
2	afternoon, autumn	2	
3	light-hearted	2	
4	simile	2	
5	Logs tripped him up. Trees took on ugly crouching shapes. It began to get dark.	3	Answers can be in any order.
6	The light seemed to be draining away like flood-water	2	

English Comprehension Standard Introductory Set Two Answers

Question number	Answer	Mark	Parent's notes and additional comments
7	hundreds of faces	2	
8	holes in the ground	2	
9	malice, hatred, hard-eyed, evil, sharp	5	Answers can be in any order.
10	He swung off the paths and plunged into the untrodden places of the wood.	3	
11	It made him hurry forward. It made him hesitate. He halted.	3	Answers can be in any order.
12	He was alone. He was unarmed. He was far from help. Night was closing in.	4	Answers can be in any order.
13	It sounded like the noise falling leaves make.	2	
14	The rabbit disappeared. …**6**… The rabbit warned Mole. …5… A rabbit ran towards Mole. …3… The pattering made a steady beat. …1… Mole waited. …4… Mole listened anxiously. …2…	5	No mark given for **6** as this was given in the question.
15	Rat was the friend who found Mole	2	
16 a	slight and delicate	2	line 38
16 b	till from every quarter	2	line 42
16 c	As he stood still to hearken	2	lines 43 - 44
16 d	slacken pace	2	line 45

www.tutormaster-services.co.uk
© 2015 Tutor Master Services

www.tutormaster-services.co.uk

Answers to Paper 2E

Question number	Answer	Mark	Parent's notes and additional comments
1	a horse	2	
2	evening or night time	2	
3	lounged into the stable for a gossip	2	
4	a horse	2	
5	a) uncomfortable b) restless c) cough(ing) d) they could hardly breathe.	4	
6	I listened and heard a soft, rushing sort of noise and a low crackling and snapping.	2	
7	a) it made them tremble b) they woke up (were awake) c) they were pulling at their halters d) they were stamping	4	
8	a) he burst into the stable b) he began to untie the horses c) he tried to lead them out	3	
9	He was in a hurry. He was frightened himself and that frightened the horses. He tried to drag the horses out by force but they would not move.	3	Use discretion to award marks for something similar.
10	a) quietly b) quickly	2	
11	James's voice is described as "quiet" and "cheery". This is likely to quieten the horses down, making them calmer, less restless, less scared and easier to move from the stable.	4	Use discretion to award marks for something similar.
12	James took off his scarf. …2… James patted the horse. …4… James led the horse out of the stable. …6… James shouted. **…8…** James coaxed the horse. …5… James tied the scarf over the horse's eyes. …3… James slipped the scarf off the horse's eyes. …7… James put on the bridle. …1…	7	

Question number	Answer	Mark	Parent's notes and additional comments
13	dashed	2	
14	When Ginger heard the neigh/noise made by Black Beauty she knew he was already safe and outside the stable. This gave Ginger courage to come out too.	3	Use discretion to award marks for something similar.
15	The horses and the fire engine.	2	
16 a	He tried us all by turns	2	line 29
16 b	flames were playing round the trap door	2	lines 36 - 37
16 c	above all the stir and din	2	line 57

Marking scheme for Compositions

Technical Skills	Marks up to
How well does the story show evidence of a clear beginning, middle and end?	5
How well does the story give a sense of completion?	5
How well has punctuation been used (including paragraphing)?	5
How accurate is the spelling?	5
Overall impression of presentation (neatness, legibility, correction of errors, etc.).	2

Content and Quality	Marks up to
How well does the story reflect the requirements of the title given?	5
How well has the candidate used descriptive techniques, e.g., adjectives, adverbs, similes, to enhance the story?	6
How well has direct speech been used and punctuated correctly?	6
How well have the feelings of the character(s) been described?	5
How coherent is the story, i.e., does it flow from beginning to end?	3
Discretionary marks awarded for overall impression of the story's effectiveness.	3

Marking scheme for Letters

Technical Skills	Marks up to
Are the address and date placed correctly?	2
Appropriate salutation reflecting the type of letter and person addressed, e.g., Dear Sir/Madam etc.	2
How well does the letter show evidence of a suitable introduction/beginning, middle and end?	4
How well does the letter give a sense of completion?	5
Has the writer signed off the letter in a manner appropriate to the recipient, i.e., in a formal or informal manner?	2
How well has punctuation been used (including paragraphing)?	5
How accurate is the spelling?	5
Overall impression of presentation (neatness, legibility, correction of errors, etc.).	2

Content and Quality	Marks up to
How well does the letter reflect the requirements of the title given?	5
How well has the candidate covered the three areas suggested in the task advice?	9 (3 per area)
Is an attempt made to address the recipient using appropriate language, i.e., formal (standard English) or informal (non-standard English)?	3
How coherent is the letter, i.e., does it flow?	3
Discretionary marks for overall impression of the letter's effectiveness in achieving the task set.	3

For more detailed advice and practical help with understanding punctuation, punctuation for direct speech and layout for letter writing and reports, see *Tutor Master helps you Learn English – A Literacy Dictionary*.

Marking scheme for Speech Conversations

Technical Skills	Marks up to
Consistent use of capital letters to begin the words that are spoken.	3
Consistent use of speech marks (" ") to enclose words that are spoken.	3
Consistent use of final pair of speech marks to enclose other punctuation marks, e.g., full stops, exclamation and question marks.	3
Consistent use of a new line used for each new speaker.	5
Consistent use of commas to separate words that are spoken from those unspoken.	4
How accurate is the spelling?	5
Overall impression of presentation (neatness, legibility, correction of errors, etc.).	2

Content and Quality	Marks up to
How well does the conversation reflect the requirements of the title given?	5
How coherent is the conversation, i.e., does it flow from beginning to end?	3
Does the conversation read/sound realistic?	2
How well does the conversation give a sense of completion?	3
How well have a variety of 'verbs of saying' been used by the speakers, e.g., said, replied, suggested, etc.?	5
How well have adverbs been used to convey the sense of expression of the speaker, e.g., replied happily, spoke sadly?	4
Discretionary marks for overall impression of the conversation's effectiveness in achieving the task set.	3

Marking scheme for Report

Technical Skills	Marks up to
How well does the report show evidence of a clear beginning, middle and end?	5
How well does the report give a sense of completion?	5
How well has punctuation been used (including paragraphing)?	5
How accurate is the spelling?	5
Overall impression of presentation (neatness, legibility, correction of errors, etc.).	2

Content and Quality	Marks up to
How well does the report reflect the requirements of the title given?	5
Is there evidence of originality of ideas that goes beyond reflecting the information set out in the reading passage?	5
How well has the candidate covered the three areas suggested in the task advice?	9 (3 per area)
How coherent is the report, i.e., does it flow from beginning to end?	5
Discretionary marks for overall impression of the report's effectiveness in achieving the task set.	4

Notes